CANTERBURY
TRAVEL GUIDE 2025

Must-See Sights, Cozy Stays, and Insider Tips for an Unforgettable Escape

Julio Coder

CANTERBURY TRAVEL GUIDE 2025

COPYRIGHT © 2025 BY JULIO CODER

All rights reserved. Except for brief quotations included in critical reviews and certain other noncommercial uses allowed by copyright law, no part of this publication may be reproduced, distributed, or transmitted in any form or by any means, including photocopying, recording, or other electronic or mechanical methods, without the publisher's prior written permission.

CANTERBURY TRAVEL GUIDE 2025

TABLE OF CONTENTS

CHAPTER ONE: WELCOME TO CANTERBURY

CHAPTER TWO: GETTING TO AND AROUND CANTERBURY

CHAPTER THREE: TOP ATTRACTIONS AND HISTORIC LANDMARKS

CHAPTER FOUR: MUSEUMS, ART, AND CULTURE

CHAPTER FIVE: HIDDEN GEMS AND LESSER-KNOWN SPOTS

CHAPTER SIX: CANTERBURY'S CULINARY SCENE

CHAPTER SEVEN: WHERE TO STAY: FROM COZY TO CHIC

CANTERBURY TRAVEL GUIDE 2025

CHAPTER EIGHT: OUTDOOR ACTIVITIES AND DAY TRIPS

CHAPTER NINE: SHOPPING AND LOCAL FINDS

CHAPTER TEN: CONCLUSION: PLANNING THE PERFECT CANTERBURY ESCAPE

CHAPTER ONE: WELCOME TO CANTERBURY

Welcome to Canterbury
Nestled in the heart of Kent, in the southeastern corner of England, Canterbury is a city where time intertwines with legend, where cobbled streets echo the footsteps of medieval pilgrims, and where an ancient cathedral still stands as a beacon of history, culture, and spirituality. Whether you're a history enthusiast, a literary buff, a lover of architecture, or simply seeking a quintessentially English experience, Canterbury offers a rich and immersive journey through the ages.

From its Roman roots to its medieval grandeur, Canterbury has long been a place of convergence—of people, ideas, religion, and art. In 2025, the city continues to captivate visitors not only with its historic treasures but also with its evolving identity as a dynamic cultural hub, seamlessly blending old-world charm with modern innovation.

A Brief History and Cultural Overview

Roman Foundations and Early Settlements

Canterbury's origins date back to the Iron Age, but it was the Romans who laid the foundations of the city we see today. Known then as Durovernum Cantiacorum, it became an important settlement after the Roman invasion in AD 43. The Romans constructed walls, roads, and public baths—some remnants of which can still be seen today, especially in the Canterbury Roman Museum.

After the fall of the Roman Empire, Canterbury became a focal point for Anglo-Saxon settlers and a key location in the Kingdom of Kent. In 597, the arrival of St. Augustine, sent by Pope Gregory the Great to convert the Anglo-Saxons, marked a turning point in British history. Augustine established a monastery and began the construction of a cathedral that would become the spiritual center of the Church of England.

Medieval Canterbury and Pilgrimage

The medieval period was Canterbury's golden era, particularly following the martyrdom of Archbishop Thomas Becket in 1170. Becket's assassination inside Canterbury Cathedral, ordered indirectly by King Henry II, sent shockwaves through Christendom. Miracles were soon reported at his tomb, and pilgrims from across Europe began to arrive in droves. This pilgrimage tradition was immortalized by Geoffrey Chaucer in his 14th-century literary masterpiece, The Canterbury Tales.

During this time, Canterbury flourished as a bustling hub of religion, commerce, and scholarship. The cathedral, reconstructed in the Gothic style after a devastating fire in 1174, became one of the most magnificent in Europe.

Tudor Reforms and Civil War

The 16th century brought seismic changes. Under Henry VIII, the English Reformation swept through Canterbury. Becket's shrine was destroyed in 1538, monasteries were dissolved, and the city's religious institutions were drastically altered. However, the cathedral remained a central symbol of the Anglican Church.

During the English Civil War in the 17th century, Canterbury sided with the Royalists. Following the war, the city saw a period of decline, but its heritage endured.

Modern Canterbury
Today, Canterbury is a vibrant university city, home to the University of Kent and Canterbury Christ Church University. It maintains its medieval layout, with timber-framed buildings, winding streets, and its iconic cathedral at the heart. The city attracts nearly a million visitors a year and continues to thrive as a cultural, educational, and spiritual center.

Why Visit Canterbury in 2025

1. UNESCO World Heritage Site and Cathedral Restoration

Canterbury Cathedral, a UNESCO World Heritage Site, has recently completed an extensive multi-million-pound restoration project in early 2025. The restoration, focused on the nave, stained glass, and cloisters, has revitalized the cathedral, enhancing accessibility and visitor experience. State-of-the-art lighting now illuminates the intricate medieval architecture, and new interpretive exhibits tell the stories of key figures such as Thomas Becket and Archbishop Lanfranc.

Guided tours, digital installations, and immersive soundscapes have been added to help visitors experience the cathedral's spiritual atmosphere like never before. Don't miss the newly restored Chapter House, which is now open to the public after years of careful conservation.

2. The Reimagined Pilgrims' Way Experience

In 2025, Canterbury has reintroduced and expanded its "Pilgrims' Way" initiative, a modern walking route inspired by the medieval pilgrimage trail. This updated route connects Winchester to Canterbury, offering waymarked paths, eco-friendly accommodations, and interactive digital guides.

As a visitor, you can walk sections of this historic trail while learning about its spiritual and literary significance. QR-code signage now links to real-time content, including readings from The Canterbury Tales, ecological notes, and historic commentary. New heritage funding in 2025 has also supported the creation of rest stops themed around Chaucer's characters.

3. Festivals and Events in 2025

Canterbury's event calendar in 2025 is packed with cultural highlights:

Canterbury Festival 2025 (October): One of the UK's most celebrated arts festivals, featuring theatre, classical music, comedy, and visual arts. This year's theme is "Echoes of the Past," with a special focus on storytelling through the ages.

Becket Week (July 5–12): Marking the anniversary of Thomas Becket's translation, the city hosts re-enactments, historical lectures, medieval fairs, and a torchlight procession.

Canterbury Medieval Pageant (July): A family-friendly event with knights, jesters, falconry, and parades through the city center.

Open City Nights (Monthly): Canterbury's landmarks, including Westgate Towers and St. Augustine's Abbey, stay open late with guided torch-lit tours.

4. Culinary and Craft Renaissance
Canterbury's food scene has undergone a renaissance, with 2025 seeing a surge in

independent eateries, sustainable cafés, and farm-to-table restaurants. Highlights include:

The Pilgrim's Pantry: A new bistro inspired by medieval recipes, reimagined with a modern twist.
Cathedral Brewhouse: A craft brewery using hops grown in nearby East Kent, offering limited-run beers named after Chaucer's characters.
Canterbury Food Hall (Opening Summer 2025): Located in a restored Victorian warehouse near the train station, it features local vendors, artisan cheeses, and a rooftop terrace.

Farmers' markets are now more frequent, and many local producers offer tasting experiences, from Kentish cider to Whitstable oysters.

5. Heritage Trails and Green Tourism
In 2025, Canterbury has expanded its network of walking and cycling trails to promote sustainable tourism. The Canterbury Heritage Loop, a 12-kilometer trail, guides visitors past Roman

ruins, medieval walls, Tudor houses, and secret gardens.

Also new is the Stour River Eco Walk, a nature-focused route with interactive boards on local flora, fauna, and conservation efforts. Birdwatching points and kayak rentals make this a perfect option for eco-conscious travelers.

6. Immersive Technology and Museum Revamps

The Canterbury Roman Museum has been revamped for 2025, featuring augmented reality tours that recreate the Roman marketplace and hypocaust. The Beaney House of Art & Knowledge now includes a new exhibition on "The Myths of Medieval Canterbury," combining digital storytelling with rare manuscripts and Chaucer-themed art installations.

7. Accessibility and Infrastructure Enhancements

In response to increased visitor numbers, the city has improved its infrastructure:

- High-Speed Rail Links from London St. Pancras now take under 55 minutes.
- A new green shuttle service connects the Park & Ride to key sites across Canterbury.
- Multilingual touchscreen guides are now installed across the city's landmarks, catering to French, German, Spanish, Mandarin, and Japanese speakers.

What's New in 2025

1. The Canterbury Heritage Gateway
Opening in spring 2025, the Canterbury Heritage Gateway is a state-of-the-art visitor center located near the Westgate Towers. Designed to be the first stop for tourists, it houses a high-definition 3D city model, orientation films, and ticketing for tours and events. A special children's zone features tactile history exhibits and virtual storytelling sessions.

2. "Chaucer Reimagined" – A New Interactive Experience

A major new exhibition launched at the Beaney Museum titled "Chaucer Reimagined" lets visitors explore The Canterbury Tales like never before. Using holograms, interactive booths, and audio narration, guests can walk alongside virtual pilgrims, choosing their own path through the tales. This initiative is part of Canterbury's broader commitment to digital innovation in heritage interpretation.

3. Expansion of St. Augustine's Abbey Site

English Heritage has expanded public access to the grounds of St. Augustine's Abbey, including newly excavated areas and a reconstructed Anglo-Saxon herb garden. Audio guides now include immersive soundscapes of Gregorian chants and Anglo-Saxon poetry. A new visitor pavilion offers interpretive displays and hosts lectures and community workshops.

4. Art and Architecture Trail: "Modern Meets Medieval"

A newly inaugurated city-wide art trail titled "Modern Meets Medieval" features contemporary installations placed alongside historic landmarks. Sculptures, projection art, and light installations explore themes of time, identity, and pilgrimage. Artists from across Europe were commissioned, making this one of the most ambitious public art programs in Canterbury's history.

5. Smart Tourism and Eco Initiatives

In 2025, Canterbury has officially launched its Smart City Tourism App, which combines AR navigation, live crowd monitoring, and AI-generated tour suggestions based on user interests. Visitors can avoid busy times, discover hidden gems, and even create digital postcards.

Environmental initiatives include:

■ Expanded bike-share stations at all major attractions.

■ A new carbon offset program for overnight guests, with incentives like discounts at eco-conscious restaurants.

■ Plastic-free zones in the city center, supported by businesses offering refill stations and reusable containers.

6. Literary and Academic Events

Canterbury continues to be a center for scholarship. In 2025, the University of Kent will host the International Chaucer Conference, expected to draw literary scholars from around the world. Public lectures, open-access workshops, and student-led exhibitions will be held throughout the summer.

Conclusion

Canterbury in 2025 is more than just a preserved medieval city—it is a living, breathing destination where ancient traditions coexist with modern innovation. The city has invested in sustainable tourism, immersive experiences, and cultural revitalization, making it one of the UK's most exciting places to visit this year.

Whether you're tracing the footsteps of pilgrims, diving into the pages of Chaucer, savoring local delicacies, or exploring green spaces along the River Stour, Canterbury offers something timeless and something new.

So pack your walking shoes, bring your curiosity, and prepare to be enchanted—welcome to Canterbury, where history greets the future.

CHAPTER TWO: GETTING TO AND AROUND CANTERBURY

Transportation Options to Canterbury

Train Travel

Canterbury is served by two main railway stations: Canterbury East and Canterbury West, both within walking distance of the city center. Trains from London St Pancras International via Southeastern's High-Speed 1 service reach Canterbury West in under 55 minutes, making it the fastest option from the capital. These high-speed services typically run twice an hour during peak periods. Standard services from London Victoria and London Charing Cross are also available, taking around 1 hour 30 minutes to reach either station.

Canterbury West: Ideal for accessing the Cathedral, Westgate Towers, and University of Kent.

Canterbury East: Convenient for Christ Church University, Dane John Gardens, and the southern parts of the city.

Advance booking on trainline platforms or National Rail websites often results in cheaper fares. Railcards (16–25, Senior, Family & Friends) are accepted and can offer up to 1/3 off.

Bus and Coach Services
National Express and Megabus operate long-distance coach routes from London Victoria Coach Station and other major UK cities. Average journey time from London is approximately 2 hours, with stops at Canterbury Bus Station in the heart of the city.

Stagecoach East Kent runs regional bus services throughout Kent, linking Canterbury with towns such as Whitstable, Herne Bay, Faversham, Dover, and Ashford. The Triangle Route is a popular loop service connecting Canterbury, Herne Bay, and Whitstable.

Car Travel

Canterbury is accessible via the A2/M2 from London and the A28 from Ashford or Thanet. Travel time by car from central London is typically 1 hour 45 minutes to 2 hours, depending on traffic. Signage is clear, especially as you approach the city from any direction.

The city has a network of Park & Ride facilities (Wincheap, Sturry Road, and New Dover Road), allowing visitors to park outside the city center and take a free shuttle bus. This system is recommended due to limited central parking and traffic congestion during peak periods and weekends.

Airports

London Gatwick: Approx. 90 minutes by car or train (via London St Pancras or Victoria).

London Heathrow: Approx. 2 hours via the Elizabeth Line or Heathrow Express to London Paddington, then by Underground to St Pancras.

London City Airport: Best for business travelers; around 1 hour 40 minutes via DLR and Southeastern trains.

Kent International Airport (Manston): Closed since 2014; not currently operating commercial flights.

Southend Airport: An alternative option; around 2 hours by train and Underground connections.

Cycling Routes to Canterbury

The National Cycle Route 1 (NCR 1) passes through Canterbury, connecting it to Whitstable and Dover. The Crab and Winkle Way, a popular 7.6-mile route from Whitstable to Canterbury, is part of this network and provides a scenic traffic-free path for cyclists.

Bicycle storage is available at both train stations and the Park & Ride sites.

Ferry Connections

Travelers arriving via the Port of Dover (around 17 miles from Canterbury) can connect easily by train, bus, or taxi. Dover is a major ferry terminal for crossings from Calais and Dunkirk, France.

Navigating the City Center and Beyond

Walking in Canterbury

The compact layout of Canterbury's historic core makes it ideal for exploring on foot. Most major attractions—including Canterbury Cathedral, The Marlowe Theatre, The Beaney House of Art & Knowledge, and Westgate Gardens—are within a 15-minute walk of each other.

Pedestrianized streets such as the High Street, St. Peter's Street, and Burgate enhance walkability, and signage is clear and multilingual in major zones. The City Centre Walking Trail, available as a printed guide or app, leads visitors through key historic sites in under two hours.

Guided Walking Tours

■ Canterbury Guided Tours offers daily historical walks departing from the Buttermarket outside the Cathedral Gate.
■ The Canterbury Ghost Tour departs nightly and explores the city's haunted alleys and medieval lore.

Bus Services Within Canterbury

Stagecoach East Kent runs a reliable intra-city bus network, with primary routes radiating from Canterbury Bus Station on St. George's Lane. Buses connect residential areas to the city center and run frequent services to surrounding towns.

Key local routes:

UniBus U1: Connects the University of Kent, city center, and Canterbury East.
Triangle Buses: Link Whitstable, Herne Bay, and Canterbury on a circular route.
Route 4 and 6: Frequent services to Thanet towns and shopping areas.

Fares range from £2 for a single to £5 for a day ticket, with contactless payment available onboard.

Taxis and Ride-Sharing

Taxis are available at designated ranks at Canterbury West, Canterbury East, and the city center (Rose Lane and St. Peter's Place). Local taxi firms such as Longley's, Green Light, and Canterbury Cars offer pre-booked services via phone or app.

Uber operates in the area, although availability may be lower than in larger cities. Expect to wait longer for rides during evenings and weekends.

Cycling Within the City

Canterbury is bike-friendly, with dedicated cycle lanes and shared-use paths. The Canterbury Cycle Map is available at tourist centers and online. Rental options include:

Kent Cycle Hire: Daily and weekly hire, located near Canterbury West.

Canterbury Bike Hire: Offers electric bikes and standard bikes with helmet and lock included.

■ Ofo dockless bikes (rebranded in 2024 under local operators) can be picked up across the city using a smartphone app.

Helmets are not legally required but are strongly advised. Most of the city center is low-speed, and bike racks are located at key tourist points.

River Navigation and Boat Tours

The River Stour provides a unique view of Canterbury via punting or small boat tours. Operators like Canterbury Historic River Tours and Westgate Punts run from spring through autumn. Tours typically last 30–45 minutes and offer commentary on the city's medieval and ecclesiastical heritage.

Parking, Accessibility, and Local Tips

Car Parking

Parking in central Canterbury is limited and can be expensive. Use of Park & Ride facilities is strongly encouraged.

City Center Car Parks:

Whitefriars Car Park (CT1 2TF): Multi-story, close to the High Street; approx. £2.50/hour.
Queningate Car Park (CT1 1YW): Smaller, close to the Cathedral precincts.
St. Radigund's Car Park (CT1 2AA): 24/7 access, close to Kingsmead Leisure Centre.
Castle Row Car Park (CT1 2PT): Convenient for Dane John Gardens.

All car parks offer contactless and app-based payment, including RingGo and JustPark. Prices range from £1.60 to £2.80 per hour. Free parking is rare within the inner city.

Park & Ride

Canterbury's three Park & Ride sites are located on Wincheap Road, New Dover Road, and Sturry Road.

■ Open daily from 7:00 am to 7:30 pm.
■ Shuttles every 10–15 minutes.
■ Parking + bus for up to 7 people: £4 per vehicle per day.
■ EV charging stations available at all locations.

The service is accessible, with wheelchair ramps, priority seating, and real-time app tracking for all routes.

Accessibility

Canterbury is steadily improving accessibility across public areas, transport, and heritage sites. Key developments in 2025 include:

■ Step-free access at both railway stations and all Park & Ride shuttles.
■ Hearing loops installed at key attractions and museums.

■ Accessible toilets located at The Beaney, Whitefriars, and Marlowe Arcade.
■ Mobility scooter hire available at Canterbury Shopmobility, Whitefriars Shopping Centre.

The Cathedral now features step-free visitor routes, new elevators to the crypt and chapter house, and virtual guides with British Sign Language interpretation. Most museums, including the Roman Museum and The Beaney, are fully accessible.

Local Tips for Visitors

Weather: Pack a waterproof jacket and layers. Canterbury's coastal climate can change quickly.
Currency: GBP (£). Most vendors accept contactless payments and mobile wallets.
Language: English is spoken, but many signs and guides are available in French, German, Mandarin, and Spanish.
Wi-Fi: Free public Wi-Fi is available in the city center via "Canterbury City WiFi."

Tourist Info: The main Visitor Information Centre is located in the Beaney House on High Street.

Safety and Security
Canterbury is considered a safe city, but common sense precautions apply. Emergency services can be reached by dialing 999 (emergency) or 101 (non-emergency police). The Canterbury Street Pastors operate on Friday and Saturday nights to assist late-night visitors.

Eco-Friendly Travel Tips

■ Carry a refillable water bottle; free water refill stations are located throughout the city.
■ Use the Canterbury Green Travel App to track low-traffic walking routes and avoid busy times.
■ Local businesses displaying the "Green Canterbury" badge follow sustainability best practices, including reduced waste and ethical sourcing.

Final Word

Canterbury in 2025 is highly navigable, with a modern transport infrastructure, pedestrian-friendly layout, and ongoing sustainability efforts. Whether you arrive by train, bike, or car, moving around is intuitive and visitor-focused. Embracing both historic charm and cutting-edge connectivity, Canterbury is designed to welcome travelers of all abilities and preferences.

CHAPTER THREE: TOP ATTRACTIONS AND HISTORIC LANDMARKS

Canterbury Cathedral and Cathedral Precincts

Canterbury Cathedral is undoubtedly the most iconic landmark in the city, attracting millions of visitors annually. As one of the oldest and most famous Christian structures in England, the Cathedral stands as a testament to the city's religious and architectural heritage.

History and Significance:

Canterbury Cathedral is the seat of the Archbishop of Canterbury, the spiritual leader of the Church of England and the worldwide Anglican Communion. The Cathedral was founded in 597 AD by St. Augustine of Canterbury, the first Archbishop of Canterbury, making it one of the oldest Christian structures in England. The current building, however, dates primarily from the 11th to 15th centuries, with notable alterations and additions made over the centuries. In 1170, the cathedral became a site of pilgrimage following the murder of Thomas Becket, the Archbishop of Canterbury, in its grounds. Becket's shrine attracted pilgrims from across Europe, making Canterbury a major religious center until the shrine was destroyed in 1538 during the reign of Henry VIII.

Architectural Features:

The Cathedral is a stunning example of Gothic architecture, with intricate stone carvings, beautiful stained glass windows, and soaring arches. Key features include:

The Nave: A vast and awe-inspiring space that stretches toward the high altar. The impressive ceiling vaulting is one of the most significant aspects of the building.

The Quire: A richly decorated area with remarkable wood carvings and a central location for daily services.

The Crypt: Dating from the Norman period, the crypt houses the tomb of St. Thomas Becket, who was canonized shortly after his death.

The Chapter House: Where the canons of the Cathedral used to meet, this room is known for its remarkable stonework and intricate carvings.

Visiting the Cathedral:

Visitors to the Cathedral can explore its interior, which is open to the public daily. Key highlights include the tombs of monarchs, such as Henry IV, as well as the stunning stained-glass windows and the famous Thomas Becket Memorial. Guided tours are available, providing in-depth historical context about the significance of the cathedral's architecture and its role in British history.

The Cathedral Precincts, the green space surrounding the Cathedral, provide a peaceful setting for reflection. Visitors can explore the College Court, The Cloisters, and the Parker's Piece Garden, which offer fantastic views of the Cathedral from various angles. The Cathedral shop and the The Undercroft Restaurant provide opportunities to relax and take in the beauty of the surrounding area.

Key Events and Services:
Canterbury Cathedral remains a place of Christian worship and pilgrimage. Services, including daily Eucharist and Evensong, are held regularly, and visitors are welcome to attend. Major events include the Canterbury Festival, an annual celebration of arts and culture, and Christmas and Easter services, which draw large congregations.

Access and Facilities:
The Cathedral is wheelchair accessible and offers a range of facilities for visitors, including a café, shop, and restroom facilities. There is also a Canterbury Cathedral App providing digital guides for a self-led tour experience.

St. Augustine's Abbey and St. Martin's Church

St. Augustine's Abbey is one of the most significant historical sites in Canterbury and forms part of the Canterbury World Heritage Site, along with Canterbury Cathedral and St. Martin's Church. Established in 598 AD by St. Augustine, this site was originally a Benedictine monastery and one of the first monastic foundations in England.

History of St. Augustine's Abbey:
The Abbey was established by St. Augustine at the request of Pope Gregory I, who sent him to England to convert the Anglo-Saxons to Christianity. It became a powerful and influential monastic center over the centuries and was pivotal in the early spread of Christianity in England. The abbey was expanded and rebuilt several times until it was dissolved in 1538 during the reign of Henry VIII, as part of his dissolution of the monasteries. The Abbey was subsequently left in ruins, but its significance remains high due to its association with early Christian history in England.

Architectural Remains:
Today, the Abbey is primarily in a state of ruin, but it is still possible to see significant portions of its structure, including the foundations of the Abbey Church, the cloisters, and the Chapter House. The site also contains St. Augustine's Tomb, which has been an important pilgrimage site for centuries.

Archaeological excavations over the years have revealed the abbey's former grandeur, with remnants of buildings, walls, and mosaics that provide insight into the Abbey's former life. Visitors can also explore the Visitor Centre, which offers exhibits detailing the Abbey's history and the role it played in early English Christianity.

St. Martin's Church:
Just a short distance from the Abbey is St. Martin's Church, which remains active today as a parish church. It is one of the oldest churches still in use in England, with parts of the building dating back to the 6th century. The church was

originally built as part of St. Augustine's mission to convert the Anglo-Saxons and is closely associated with his work in Kent.

St. Martin's Church contains several important historical features, including:

■ Roman brickwork in the walls, which suggests it was built using materials from nearby Roman structures.

■ Early Christian artwork and features inside the church, including ancient altars and stained glass windows.

■ The Tomb of Queen Bertha, who was the Christian wife of the Anglo-Saxon King Æthelberht of Kent and an important figure in early Christian history in England.

Visiting St. Augustine's Abbey and St. Martin's Church:
St. Augustine's Abbey is open year-round to visitors, offering an immersive experience into early English Christianity. The visitor center provides a fascinating overview of the Abbey's history, and a peaceful walk through the ruins

offers a connection to the past. St. Martin's Church is still an active parish church, and visitors are welcome to explore its interior, attend services, or simply admire the historical surroundings.

Westgate Towers and the City Walls
The Westgate Towers and the City Walls are integral to Canterbury's medieval character, providing a glimpse into the city's history as a fortified settlement.

Westgate Towers:
The Westgate Towers, built in the 14th century, are one of the most complete medieval gates in England. Originally constructed to protect the western entrance to the city, the towers were part of Canterbury's defensive walls and served as a key entry point for both locals and pilgrims.

History and Significance:
The Westgate Towers were built during the reign of King Edward III and were designed to protect the city from potential invaders, including during

the Wars of the Roses. Over the centuries, the Westgate Towers also functioned as a prison for those who broke the law in Canterbury. Today, the towers are a symbol of the city's medieval history, and the structure remains largely intact.

Architectural Features:
The towers are composed of two large gatehouses, each with a distinct architectural style. The gates were originally reinforced with drawbridges and large wooden doors, remnants of which can still be seen. The interior features several rooms and exhibits related to the history of the towers and the city's defenses. The Westgate Museum located within the towers showcases historical artifacts from medieval Canterbury and the prison's history.

City Walls:
The City Walls of Canterbury date back to Roman times but were heavily modified and expanded during the medieval period. The walls once encircled the entire city, providing defense against invaders and helping to control the flow

of people into and out of Canterbury. Today, visitors can walk along parts of the surviving walls, taking in panoramic views of the city and surrounding countryside.

Key Sections of the Walls:
■ The Roman Walls: Remnants of the original Roman walls can still be seen at the Tannery Lane section.
■ The Medieval Walls: Later walls, which encircle the Canterbury Christ Church University and St. George's Street, offer excellent views of the city.
■ The Walls at Dane John Gardens: One of the best-preserved sections, with pathways allowing for a scenic walk along the ancient walls.

Visiting Westgate Towers and the City Walls:
Westgate Towers are open to the public and feature interactive exhibits, including medieval prison cells and displays about the tower's history. The surrounding Westgate Gardens offer a peaceful place for visitors to relax. The City Walls can be explored on foot, with several

walking routes that follow the ancient fortifications.

There are also guided tours of the City Walls that provide in-depth historical context. The City Wall Trail leads visitors on a circular route around Canterbury, highlighting significant locations along the walls and offering a glimpse into how the city evolved from its Roman origins to its medieval peak.

Conclusion

Canterbury is a city rich in history and culture, with a vast array of landmarks that tell the story of its development over the centuries. From the grandeur of Canterbury Cathedral and the surrounding precincts to the ruins of St. Augustine's Abbey and the medieval defenses of the Westgate Towers, visitors are offered a unique opportunity to explore the past and witness the continuing legacy of Canterbury as one of England's most important historical and religious centers.

CHAPTER FOUR: MUSEUMS, ART, AND CULTURE

The Beaney House of Art & Knowledge

The Beaney House of Art & Knowledge is one of Canterbury's most significant cultural institutions, offering a rich blend of art, history, and knowledge. This Victorian building, dating back to 1899, houses collections spanning visual arts, local history, and educational resources, providing visitors with a comprehensive understanding of the city's heritage and cultural evolution.

History and Significance:

The Beaney House was originally established as a public museum and library, funded by the legacy of Sir Thomas Beaney, a local philanthropist. Its purpose was to foster art and education within the community. Over the years, it has undergone numerous expansions and refurbishments to enhance its offerings, becoming a vital hub for cultural engagement. Today, it is a Grade II-listed building, reflecting its historical importance.

Collections and Exhibitions:
The Beaney is home to a diverse collection that spans across several key themes:

Fine Art: The art collection includes works from the 18th to 20th centuries, with a particular focus on Victorian and Edwardian pieces. Visitors can find paintings, sculptures, and drawings by local artists as well as pieces from notable national and international artists.

Local History and Archaeology: The museum houses fascinating exhibits about Canterbury's history, from its Roman roots to its development as a medieval city. This includes collections of ancient artifacts, archaeological finds, and historical documents that tell the story of Canterbury's evolution.

Temporary Exhibitions: The Beaney regularly hosts rotating exhibitions, which can include contemporary art, photography, and thematic historical displays. These temporary exhibitions offer a fresh perspective on art and culture and provide space for local and international artists to showcase their work.

Visitor Experience:
The Beaney is centrally located in the heart of Canterbury, making it easily accessible for tourists and locals alike. Its modern facilities, combined with its historical architecture, create a welcoming environment for exploration. The museum also features an interactive section for children, making it a family-friendly destination. The museum's café offers a perfect place to relax, enjoy light refreshments, and take in the surrounding atmosphere. Its shop provides a wide selection of books, art materials, and locally themed souvenirs, allowing visitors to take home a piece of Canterbury's cultural heritage.

Key Events and Programs:
The Beaney frequently organizes events and programs that cater to a wide audience. These include art workshops, historical talks,

educational sessions for school groups, and family-oriented activities. In addition, the museum plays host to special events during cultural festivals like the Canterbury Festival, which celebrates the arts, music, and performance in the city.

Access and Facilities:
The Beaney is wheelchair accessible and provides a variety of services, including free Wi-Fi, guided tours, and educational resources. It is also a popular venue for community engagement and cultural education, offering school visits and community outreach programs.

Canterbury Roman Museum
Canterbury Roman Museum is dedicated to showcasing the city's Roman past, offering an in-depth exploration of Canterbury's transformation from a small Roman settlement into the thriving city of Durovernum Cantiacorum. The museum offers visitors a chance to step back in time and discover the

fascinating history of the Roman period in Canterbury.

History and Significance:
Canterbury's history as a Roman settlement dates back to the 1st century AD, when the Romans established Durovernum Cantiacorum as a key administrative center in Roman Britain. The city was an important military and civilian hub, and its strategic location near the Roman road network made it a focal point of trade, culture, and administration. The museum is situated near the Roman baths and mosaic floors, with some exhibits coming from the direct excavations of Roman remains within the city.

Museum Layout and Collections:
The Canterbury Roman Museum offers a range of exhibits that provide insight into daily life during Roman times. Visitors can explore:

Roman Artifacts: The museum's collection of Roman pottery, tools, and everyday items offers a glimpse into the domestic lives of Romans living in Canterbury. Notable items include pottery from the local area, military equipment, and coins that illustrate the city's trade connections.

Roman Mosaics: The museum is famous for its extensive collection of Roman mosaics, including some beautifully preserved floor mosaics that were originally part of wealthy Roman homes. These intricate works of art depict scenes from mythology, nature, and daily life.

Roman Baths: One of the key attractions is the preserved Roman bathhouse, which gives visitors an idea of the sophisticated bathing culture of the Romans. The bathhouse includes interactive displays that explain the various stages of the Roman bathing process and the importance of public baths in Roman society.

Roman Military Life: Exhibits also focus on the military presence in the city, exploring the role of the Roman army and its impact on the development of Canterbury. Visitors can view artifacts such as weapons, armor, and military uniforms used by Roman soldiers.

Thematic Exhibitions: Temporary exhibitions often focus on specific aspects of Roman life, such as trade, religion, or the construction of Roman infrastructure.

Visitor Experience:

The museum is designed to engage visitors of all ages, with interactive displays and immersive exhibits. Key highlights include a virtual reality experience that allows visitors to see a digital recreation of Roman Canterbury, bringing the city's ancient streets and buildings to life. Additionally, the Roman Baths Experience provides a hands-on look at the bathing ritual, with real and replica artifacts.

The museum is located near the High Street, making it easy to incorporate into a day of sightseeing in Canterbury. Guided tours are available for those wishing to learn more about the Roman era in depth, and there are educational programs for school groups.

Key Events and Programs:

The museum runs special events throughout the year, including workshops on Roman crafts, archaeology digs, and lectures on Roman history. During the summer months, visitors can enjoy themed activities such as Roman re-enactments, where actors in Roman costume bring history to life through interactive performances.

Access and Facilities:
The museum is wheelchair accessible, with ramps and lifts to ensure all visitors can explore the exhibits. It offers educational programs tailored to students, families, and archaeology enthusiasts, and the shop features Roman-themed gifts, books, and souvenirs.

Local Galleries, Events, and Performances
Canterbury is home to a vibrant arts scene, with a range of local galleries, performance spaces, and cultural events that reflect the city's artistic heritage and contemporary creativity.

Local Art Galleries:

Canterbury boasts a variety of galleries that showcase both contemporary and classical works, often focusing on local and regional artists.

Canterbury Contemporary: Located in the city center, Canterbury Contemporary is an innovative space that features a rotating selection of contemporary art exhibitions. The gallery often hosts group shows and solo exhibitions by emerging artists. It is a focal point for cutting-edge visual art, with a particular emphasis on experimental media and interdisciplinary work.

The Sidney Cooper Gallery: This gallery is part of the Canterbury Christ Church University and showcases a range of contemporary art exhibitions, often involving students and recent graduates. The gallery hosts regular events, including workshops, artist talks, and group exhibitions.

The Turner Contemporary: While not technically located in Canterbury, the Turner Contemporary in nearby Margate is an influential art venue for the region, often featuring works by major British and international artists.

Local Cultural Events:
Canterbury's cultural calendar is packed with events that celebrate the arts and local talent.

The Canterbury Festival: Held annually in October, this festival is the city's premier arts and culture event, drawing thousands of visitors. It features music, theater, dance, and visual arts, with performances and exhibitions held in various venues throughout the city.

Canterbury's Christmas Market: During the winter season, Canterbury hosts a magical Christmas market, offering locally made arts and crafts, seasonal performances, and festive art installations.

Music Festivals: Canterbury also plays host to a range of music festivals and live performances throughout the year, including classical concerts, jazz performances, and contemporary music events. These events are held at venues like the Canterbury Cathedral, The Gulbenkian Theatre, and various local pubs and clubs.

Performances and Theatre:
Canterbury has a rich theatrical heritage, and its theaters regularly stage a diverse range of performances.

The Marlowe Theatre: This is Canterbury's leading performance venue, offering a broad range of productions, including West End shows, classical performances, dance, and operas. The theater is named after the famous playwright Christopher Marlowe, who was born in the city.

The Gulbenkian Theatre: Associated with Canterbury Christ Church University, this theater is known for its avant-garde productions, ranging from contemporary drama to experimental performances. It also hosts regular dance and comedy events.

Theatre-in-the-Round: Canterbury is also home to smaller, more intimate venues like The Theatre-in-the-Round, which offers a chance to experience experimental theater and new works by up-and-coming playwrights.

Public Art and Installations:

Throughout the city, visitors can find public art installations and sculptures that contribute to the cultural landscape. The Canterbury Public Art Trail takes visitors on a walking route through the city's most notable outdoor artworks, showcasing the creativity and diversity of local artists.

Conclusion

Canterbury is a city where art, history, and culture come together to offer a vibrant, immersive experience for all visitors. From the Beaney House of Art & Knowledge and the Canterbury Roman Museum to local galleries and performances, there is something for every art enthusiast, history lover, and cultural explorer to enjoy. Whether you're interested in ancient Roman history, contemporary visual art, or live performances, Canterbury offers a rich and diverse cultural landscape that celebrates the city's heritage while embracing modern creativity.

CHAPTER FIVE: HIDDEN GEMS AND LESSER-KNOWN SPOTS

Greyfriars Garden and Franciscan Chapel

Greyfriars Garden, a serene and often overlooked green space in the heart of Canterbury, is a delightful spot for those seeking peace and history away from the crowds. Nestled behind Canterbury's bustling High Street, Greyfriars Garden offers a tranquil escape with historical significance dating back to medieval times. The garden is located on the site of the Greyfriars Monastery, a Franciscan friary founded in the 13th century.

Historical Significance:

Greyfriars Monastery was originally established by the Franciscan friars, who came to Canterbury in the early 13th century. The friary was part of a larger network of Franciscan communities across England. The monastery was suppressed in the 16th century during the reign of King Henry VIII as part of his dissolution of the monasteries. Today, the remains of the Franciscan Chapel, a small but evocative ruin, serve as a reminder of the once-thriving religious community. The chapel, although now in ruins, remains a poignant symbol of Canterbury's religious past.

The Garden and Its Features:
Greyfriars Garden itself is a well-maintained public space, with manicured lawns, shady trees, and a peaceful atmosphere that invites visitors to relax and reflect. The garden is divided into different sections, each with its own character. The flower beds provide vibrant color during the warmer months, while the mature trees offer shade and comfort on sunny days. A central water feature adds to the tranquility of the space, and there are several benches around the garden where visitors can sit and enjoy the surroundings.

The Franciscan Chapel ruins are a significant feature of the garden. Visitors can see the remaining walls of the chapel and imagine what it might have looked like during its prime. The ruins are often overlooked by tourists, making it a peaceful spot to enjoy Canterbury's rich medieval history without the crowds. The chapel is also associated with several legends and myths about the friars, which add an air of mystery to the site.

Accessibility and Visitor Experience:
Greyfriars Garden is open to the public year-round, and its location in the city center makes it easy to access. The garden is free to visit, making it an ideal stop for those wanting a quiet space to reflect or have a picnic. While the garden is not large, its intimate and peaceful atmosphere provides a unique opportunity to step back in time and experience a more contemplative side of Canterbury.

The Franciscan Chapel ruins are open for exploration, but visitors should be aware that they are in a partially restored state. Information boards explain the history of the friary and the significance of the chapel in the broader context of Canterbury's religious development.

Nearby Attractions:
Greyfriars Garden is conveniently located near other historical attractions, such as the Canterbury Cathedral and the St. Augustine's Abbey. Visitors can easily combine a trip to the garden with visits to these more famous landmarks. Additionally, Greyfriars Garden offers a peaceful contrast to the busy shopping streets of Canterbury, providing a refreshing break from the hustle and bustle of the city center.

Crooked House and Conquest House
Crooked House and Conquest House are two of Canterbury's more peculiar and lesser-known buildings, each with its own charm and intriguing backstory. These architectural curiosities are hidden gems that reveal more about the city's character and its long-standing architectural heritage.

Crooked House:

The Crooked House is a famous building located near the High Street in Canterbury, notable for its peculiar tilt. The structure is one of the oldest surviving timber-framed buildings in the city and is thought to date back to the early 16th century. Its distinctive tilt and lean make it appear as though the building is in danger of toppling over, giving it a unique and eye-catching appearance.

While the reason behind the building's tilt is not definitively known, it is believed to be the result of subsidence or uneven ground on which the building was constructed. The Crooked House stands as a testament to Canterbury's medieval and early modern architecture, showcasing the ingenuity and adaptability of its builders.

Architecture and Features:

The building features traditional timber framing, which was common in Canterbury and other English cities during the late medieval period. The upper floors of the Crooked House are visibly leaning, with the entire structure giving the impression of imminent collapse. The façade is a classic example of Elizabethan construction, with exposed wooden beams and a distinctive overhanging upper story that is typical of the period.

Legends and Myths:
Like many historical buildings, the Crooked House has inspired a number of local legends. One of the most persistent myths is that the house was constructed deliberately in its tilted form, possibly as a space-saving technique or to create a visual spectacle. Another legend suggests that the building was once home to a notorious local family known for their eccentricity. Although these stories are unsubstantiated, they add to the building's intrigue and mystique.

Visitor Experience:
The Crooked House is not open for tours, as it is still a privately owned building. However, it remains a popular stop for tourists taking a

walking tour of Canterbury. Its unusual appearance makes it a favorite subject for photographs, and it is often included in guides to the city's hidden treasures. Visitors can view the building from the outside and marvel at its peculiar tilt.

Conquest House:

Located just a short walk from the Crooked House is Conquest House, another lesser-known yet historically significant building in Canterbury. Conquest House is a Grade II-listed building that dates back to the 17th century. It is one of the few surviving examples of early post-medieval townhouses in Canterbury, and it showcases the architectural transition from the medieval period to the modern era. The building's most striking feature is its front façade, which combines elements of traditional timber framing with later brickwork and features Georgian-style windows.

History and Significance:

The name "Conquest House" likely refers to the Norman Conquest of England in the 11th century, a nod to the historical period during which the building was constructed. It is believed that the house was originally part of a larger group of homes belonging to Canterbury's wealthy merchants. The structure's detailed wooden beams and decorative features reflect the social status of its original inhabitants.

Architecture and Features:
The most distinctive aspect of Conquest House is its combination of medieval timber framing and later Georgian elements, including the symmetrical windows and brickwork. The house retains much of its original charm, including wooden paneling, fireplaces, and decorative moldings. Visitors can admire the building's historical craftsmanship and take note of the structural contrasts that make Conquest House such a unique example of Canterbury's evolving architectural styles.

Current Use:

Today, Conquest House is used as a private residence and is not open to the public. However, it can still be admired from the outside, and its historical significance makes it an interesting stop for those keen on exploring Canterbury's lesser-known buildings.

Tower House and the Dane John Gardens
Tower House and the Dane John Gardens are another pair of hidden gems that contribute to Canterbury's rich tapestry of history and natural beauty. Located just to the north of the city center, Tower House offers a glimpse into the city's medieval past, while the nearby Dane John Gardens provide a lush and serene setting for those looking to relax in nature.

Tower House:
Tower House is a historic building located on the edge of the Dane John Gardens, and it offers a fascinating insight into Canterbury's medieval architecture. The house is believed to have been built during the 12th century, making it one of the oldest surviving structures in the city. It is

often described as a fortified house due to its tower-like features and defensive architecture.

Historical Significance:

Tower House was likely constructed as a defensive residence for a wealthy merchant or landowner. The structure's location near the city's walls suggests it may have been used as a watchtower or fortified home during times of conflict. The thick stone walls, narrow windows, and high position above the surrounding gardens all indicate that Tower House was designed with defense in mind.

Today, the building remains privately owned and is not open for public tours, but its unique architectural style and historical importance make it an interesting site for those exploring the city's medieval past.

Dane John Gardens:

Located directly adjacent to Tower House is the Dane John Gardens, a large public park that offers a perfect blend of natural beauty and historical significance. The gardens are one of

Canterbury's oldest public parks, dating back to the 17th century. The site was originally used as a burial ground, and it was later transformed into a public garden for locals and visitors to enjoy.

Features and Attractions:
The Dane John Gardens feature beautifully manicured lawns, flowerbeds, and trees, making it an ideal place for relaxation, picnicking, or leisurely walks. The park's centerpiece is an elevated mound, which offers stunning views over the surrounding city and is the site of a medieval motte. The Dane John mound is thought to have been part of a Norman fortification used to defend Canterbury during the early Middle Ages.

The gardens also feature a historic gateway, which once served as the entrance to the medieval city, and a monument to local benefactors. Today, the Dane John Gardens are a peaceful retreat in the heart of Canterbury, offering visitors a serene escape from the city's more tourist-heavy areas.

Visitor Experience:
The gardens are open year-round and are free to enter. Visitors can enjoy a leisurely stroll around the park, explore the historical features, or simply sit and enjoy the atmosphere. The gardens are family-friendly, with plenty of space for children to play, and there are several benches where visitors can relax and enjoy the surrounding natural beauty.

Conclusion
Canterbury is a city steeped in history, and while its famous landmarks often steal the spotlight, it is the hidden gems like Greyfriars Garden, Crooked House, Conquest House, Tower House, and Dane John Gardens that truly offer a deeper connection to the city's rich past and serene beauty. These lesser-known spots provide visitors with a chance to explore the more intimate side of Canterbury, whether through its fascinating historical buildings, peaceful green spaces, or quiet, contemplative sites. For those looking to escape the crowds and discover

something truly unique, these hidden gems offer a rewarding and enriching experience.

CHAPTER SIX: CANTERBURY'S CULINARY SCENE

Top-Rated Restaurants and Local Favorites
Canterbury boasts a thriving culinary scene that reflects its rich history and diverse culture. From fine dining to cozy bistros, the city offers a wide variety of dining experiences for all tastes and budgets. Here's a deep dive into some of the top-rated restaurants and local favorites that make Canterbury a food lover's paradise.

1. The Ambrette
The Ambrette is one of Canterbury's most celebrated fine dining establishments, known for its modern take on Indian cuisine. Located near the city center, this restaurant blends traditional Indian flavors with local British ingredients, creating a menu that is both inventive and refined. The Ambrette is particularly famous for its tasting menus, which feature a range of small

dishes that showcase the best of Indian cuisine with a contemporary twist.

Signature Dishes:
Some standout dishes at The Ambrette include the 'Saffron Scallops', the 'Goan-style Salmon', and the 'Lamb Shank Rogan Josh'. The restaurant's use of locally sourced produce and sustainable seafood ensures that each dish is as fresh as it is flavorful.

Dining Experience:
The ambiance at The Ambrette is sophisticated yet welcoming. The minimalist decor and intimate setting create a relaxed environment where guests can enjoy an unhurried meal. The service is attentive, and the knowledgeable staff are happy to guide diners through the extensive wine list and offer recommendations to complement their meal.

2. Café des Amis
For those seeking a cozy yet refined dining experience, Café des Amis is a must-visit. This

French bistro-style restaurant specializes in hearty, classic French dishes made with the finest seasonal ingredients. Located just a short walk from Canterbury Cathedral, Café des Amis offers a menu that includes everything from fresh seafood to rich French stews.

Signature Dishes:
The restaurant is particularly well-known for its 'Duck Confit', which is slow-cooked to perfection and served with a delicious orange glaze. Other favorites include the 'Moules Marinières' (mussels cooked in white wine) and the 'Beef Bourguignon', a rich and comforting French classic.

Dining Experience:
Café des Amis is renowned for its relaxed yet sophisticated atmosphere. With wooden floors, soft lighting, and French artwork adorning the walls, the setting is charming and intimate. The menu is complemented by an extensive list of French wines, making it an ideal choice for wine enthusiasts.

3. The Goods Shed

The Goods Shed is a unique and vibrant food market and restaurant located in a former railway shed. It's a hub for food lovers, offering a variety of fresh produce, meats, cheeses, and baked goods from local farmers and artisans. The Goods Shed also features a restaurant that serves dishes made with the best local ingredients available.

Signature Dishes:

While the menu changes seasonally, the 'Pork Belly with Cider Sauce' and 'Fish of the Day' (which often includes fresh, local catch) are standout items. The 'House-made Sausages', paired with seasonal vegetables, are also a local favorite.

Dining Experience:

The Goods Shed offers a laid-back and casual dining experience. The restaurant's open kitchen allows diners to watch the chefs at work, and the bustling atmosphere of the food market adds a lively energy to the experience. With a range of food options and a variety of seating choices, The Goods Shed is perfect for everything from a casual lunch to a more formal dinner.

4. The Marlowe Theatre Restaurant

For an elegant dining experience, The Marlowe Theatre Restaurant offers pre-theatre dining in a stylish setting. The restaurant is located next to Canterbury's iconic Marlowe Theatre, making it the perfect spot for those attending performances or looking for a memorable meal before or after the show.

Signature Dishes:

The restaurant offers a seasonal menu with dishes that range from 'Sea Bass with Lemon Butter Sauce' to 'Slow-cooked Lamb Shoulder'. Their 'Vegan Risotto' and 'Cauliflower Steak' are also excellent choices for those seeking plant-based options.

Dining Experience:

The Marlowe Theatre Restaurant is contemporary in design, offering a chic and stylish environment with floor-to-ceiling windows that overlook the theatre district. The service is attentive, and the pre-theatre menu allows diners to enjoy a meal without feeling rushed.

5. Zizzi

For those craving Italian food, Zizzi offers a modern take on classic Italian dishes in a relaxed and family-friendly atmosphere. Located in the heart of Canterbury, Zizzi is known for its delicious pizzas, pastas, and fresh salads.

Signature Dishes:

'Rustica Pizzas' are a standout, with thin, crispy crusts and a variety of fresh toppings. The 'Linguine with King Prawns' and the 'Pollo al Forno' (oven-baked chicken) are also popular menu items.

Dining Experience:

Zizzi is ideal for casual dining, whether you're enjoying a family meal or a relaxed dinner with friends. The atmosphere is lively, and the modern decor and large windows provide a bright and welcoming space for diners.

Cafés, Bakeries, and Afternoon Tea Spots
Canterbury offers a delightful selection of cafés and bakeries, making it the perfect city for coffee lovers and afternoon tea enthusiasts. These spots offer delicious pastries, fresh-brewed coffee, and traditional afternoon tea in charming surroundings.

1. EAT
EAT is a local favorite café located on the High Street, offering a range of freshly prepared sandwiches, salads, and pastries. Known for its warm and inviting atmosphere, it's the perfect spot for breakfast, brunch, or a mid-afternoon coffee.

Signature Offerings:

The 'Eggs Benedict' and 'Croissants with Butter and Jam' are popular choices for breakfast, while the 'Carrot Cake' and 'Lemon Drizzle Cake' are favorite desserts.

Experience:
The café offers a relaxed atmosphere with a selection of cozy seating. It's a great spot for people-watching, and its prime location makes it convenient for those exploring the city.

2. The Old City Bakery
Situated just a stone's throw from Canterbury Cathedral, The Old City Bakery specializes in homemade breads, cakes, and pastries. The bakery is a family-run business that prides itself on using local, organic ingredients. The fragrant smell of freshly baked bread wafts through the streets, drawing visitors in for a taste of traditional British baking.

Signature Offerings:
The 'Sourdough Bread' and 'Chelsea Buns' are standout items. The bakery also serves a

selection of 'Afternoon Teas', which include a range of freshly made sandwiches, cakes, and scones with jam and cream.

Experience:
The Old City Bakery exudes old-world charm with its quaint, rustic interior. The service is friendly, and the café offers a relaxing space to enjoy a traditional afternoon tea or a freshly baked treat.

3. The Tea House

The Tea House, located near the city center, is a quintessential spot for anyone looking to experience a traditional English afternoon tea. This charming establishment serves a selection of over 40 different teas, along with homemade cakes and scones.

Signature Offerings:
The 'Traditional Afternoon Tea' comes with a selection of finger sandwiches, freshly baked scones with jam and cream, and a variety of

cakes. The 'Cucumber Sandwiches' and 'Victoria Sponge Cake' are local favorites.

Experience:
The Tea House has a cozy, vintage feel with its floral decor and mismatched teacups. The relaxed atmosphere and friendly staff make it the perfect place to unwind with a hot cup of tea and a delicious treat.

4. Patisserie Valerie
Patisserie Valerie, a renowned French bakery chain, has a beautiful café located on Canterbury's High Street. Famous for its traditional French pastries and cakes, it's the ideal destination for those with a sweet tooth.

Signature Offerings:
The 'Croissants', 'Macarons', and 'Eclairs' are crowd-pleasers. For something more indulgent, try the 'Chocolate Mousse Cake' or the 'Tarte aux Fruits'.

Experience:

The elegant setting, with its Parisian-inspired décor and charming atmosphere, provides the perfect backdrop for a relaxed afternoon tea or a pastry break.

Pubs, Breweries, and Evening Delights
Canterbury's nightlife is vibrant, with a wide selection of pubs, breweries, and restaurants offering a variety of local and international drinks. Whether you're looking for a cozy pub with traditional ales or a trendy bar serving craft cocktails, Canterbury has it all.

1. The Old Buttermarket
The Old Buttermarket is a historic pub located in the heart of Canterbury. Dating back to the 17th century, this traditional pub offers a wide selection of ales and ciders from local breweries.

Signature Offerings:
The pub serves a rotating selection of real ales and classic British pub fare, including 'Fish and Chips', 'Bangers and Mash', and 'Steak and Ale Pie'.

Experience:
The atmosphere is cozy and welcoming, with wooden beams and an open fireplace. The Old Buttermarket often features live music, making it a lively spot for evening drinks.

2. Canterbury Ales
For craft beer enthusiasts, Canterbury Ales is a must-visit brewery. This local brewery produces a range of beers, including lagers, IPAs, and stouts, all made using locally sourced ingredients.

Signature Offerings:
Try their signature 'Canterbury Pale Ale', a light and refreshing beer with floral notes, or the richer, malty 'Canterbury Porter'.

Experience:
The brewery offers tours and tastings, allowing visitors to learn about the brewing process while sampling a range of beers. The laid-back setting

and friendly atmosphere make it a great place to spend an evening.

3. The Dolphin Pub
Located along the River Stour, The Dolphin Pub offers a picturesque setting for enjoying a pint or two. The pub has a selection of local ales and a cozy interior with views over the river.

Signature Offerings:
Known for its 'Pub Grub', including 'Beef Burgers' and 'Cheese Platters', the Dolphin Pub is a perfect spot for a casual night out.

Experience:
With a relaxed, traditional pub vibe and a riverside terrace, The Dolphin Pub is an ideal place to enjoy a drink with friends or relax after a day of sightseeing.

Canterbury's culinary scene offers a rich variety of experiences, from top-rated restaurants and cozy cafés to historic pubs and modern breweries. Whether you're looking for fine dining, traditional afternoon tea, or a place to enjoy a pint of local ale, Canterbury has something for every palate.

CHAPTER SEVEN: WHERE TO STAY: FROM COZY TO CHIC

Boutique Hotels and Charming B&Bs

Canterbury offers a range of boutique hotels and charming bed and breakfasts that provide a cozy, intimate, and often luxurious place to stay. These accommodations are perfect for those who want to experience the city's unique character and blend of modern luxury with historic charm.

1. The Falstaff Hotel

The Falstaff Hotel is one of Canterbury's oldest hotels, offering a historic yet stylish place to stay. Located near the city center, this hotel blends old-world charm with modern amenities. With its distinctive Tudor-style building, it offers a warm and welcoming atmosphere that reflects the charm of Canterbury.

Key Features:

The Falstaff is known for its traditional design and modern comforts. Rooms are tastefully decorated with a mix of classic furniture and contemporary touches. The hotel offers an on-site restaurant serving British cuisine and a cozy bar for evening drinks. Its central location makes it a convenient base for exploring Canterbury's top attractions.

Perfect For:
Couples and history enthusiasts who appreciate the charm of staying in a historic building with modern amenities.

2. The Canterbury Hotel

The Canterbury Hotel is a boutique accommodation that offers a blend of comfort, character, and excellent service. Located just a short walk from the city center, the hotel provides easy access to Canterbury Cathedral, the Westgate Towers, and other major landmarks.

Key Features:

This hotel offers a range of rooms, from classic doubles to more luxurious suites. Guests can enjoy a relaxing stay with complimentary Wi-Fi, flat-screen TVs, and comfortable beds. The hotel also offers a hearty breakfast, perfect for starting a day of sightseeing.

Perfect For:
Visitors who want a comfortable and well-located hotel with a touch of boutique charm. It's especially great for first-time visitors to the city.

3. The Tudor House

The Tudor House is a small boutique hotel that combines historical elegance with modern amenities. Located in the heart of Canterbury, it offers a peaceful atmosphere in a building that dates back to the 15th century.

Key Features:
Each room is individually decorated, combining antique furnishings with modern conveniences. The hotel is known for its outstanding

hospitality, with friendly staff offering personalized service. The Tudor House also offers a cozy breakfast room and a beautiful garden where guests can relax.

Perfect For:
Travelers seeking a quiet, charming stay with easy access to Canterbury's main attractions. It's especially ideal for couples looking for a romantic getaway.

4. The Millers Arms

For those who enjoy staying in a place with character and a bit of history, The Millers Arms is a charming B&B that offers a more intimate and traditional experience. Situated near the River Stour and close to the city center, this hotel has an excellent reputation for its hospitality.

Key Features:
The Millers Arms offers comfortable rooms with antique furnishings and cozy décor. Its traditional English pub atmosphere makes it a

fantastic option for those who want to experience the quintessential British B&B. The pub serves traditional pub food, and the breakfast options are diverse, including a full English breakfast.

Perfect For:
Those who love the atmosphere of a traditional pub, as well as travelers looking for a personalized experience in a quiet, scenic part of Canterbury.

5. The King's Head Hotel
Located just steps from Canterbury Cathedral, the King's Head Hotel is an elegant boutique hotel housed in a Grade II listed building. This historical hotel offers stylish rooms, many of which feature period details and high ceilings.

Key Features:
The King's Head combines classic British elegance with modern luxury. It features a restaurant, a cocktail bar, and private meeting spaces. The hotel's proximity to Canterbury

Cathedral makes it a top choice for visitors exploring the city's religious and architectural history.

Perfect For:
Those who want a luxurious stay in the heart of Canterbury's historic district, offering convenience and style.

Budget-Friendly and Family Options
For travelers visiting Canterbury on a budget or those with families, there are a variety of accommodation options that cater to different needs without compromising on comfort or location.

1. Travelodge Canterbury Central
The Travelodge Canterbury Central offers affordable accommodation right in the city center, providing a convenient base for visitors who want to explore the city without breaking the bank.

Key Features:

Travelodge is known for offering basic but comfortable rooms with essential amenities like flat-screen TVs, Wi-Fi, and tea and coffee making facilities. The hotel also offers a family-friendly atmosphere with a range of room sizes and family deals. While the rooms are simple, the central location makes it ideal for those who plan to spend most of their time exploring.

Perfect For:
Budget-conscious travelers, including families or groups, looking for a no-frills, centrally located hotel with good value for money.

2. Premier Inn Canterbury City Centre

The Premier Inn Canterbury City Centre is another excellent budget option, located just a short walk from Canterbury Cathedral and other major attractions. Premier Inn is well-known for its consistency and family-friendly services.

Key Features:

Premier Inn offers comfortable rooms with modern furnishings, including family rooms that can accommodate up to four people. Rooms come equipped with Wi-Fi, flat-screen TVs, and cozy beds. The hotel also features a restaurant serving breakfast and dinner, making it convenient for families to enjoy a meal without leaving the hotel.

Perfect For:
Families, couples, and groups seeking budget-friendly accommodations with a reliable, comfortable stay near the city's main attractions.

3. Ibis Canterbury

The Ibis Canterbury is a budget hotel located just a short drive from the city center. It offers simple and comfortable accommodations with the modern amenities that make it a great choice for those looking for a practical place to stay without paying high prices.

Key Features:

Rooms at Ibis are modern and functional, with comfortable beds, flat-screen TVs, and Wi-Fi access. The hotel offers a casual atmosphere, and the on-site bar and restaurant provide guests with a relaxed dining experience. The hotel also offers family rooms, making it a great option for those traveling with children.

Perfect For:
Budget-conscious travelers who need a comfortable, no-frills stay with easy access to the city center.

4. Canterbury Cathedral Lodge

The Canterbury Cathedral Lodge offers unique, budget-friendly accommodations located within the Cathedral precincts. This lodging is part of the Canterbury Cathedral Foundation, offering a quiet, peaceful setting while still being close to the city's main attractions.

Key Features:
The rooms at the Cathedral Lodge are comfortable and modern, with stunning views of

the Cathedral. The hotel offers family rooms, and guests have access to the lovely Cathedral grounds. The breakfast options are excellent, and the hotel provides a peaceful and inspiring setting for visitors.

Perfect For:
Those looking for a unique and peaceful stay, especially families or individuals who are interested in the history and culture of Canterbury Cathedral.

5. Holiday Inn Express Canterbury

The Holiday Inn Express Canterbury offers budget-friendly accommodation with the comfort and convenience of a well-known hotel chain. Located just outside the city center, the hotel provides easy access to Canterbury's attractions and the surrounding countryside.

Key Features:
The rooms at Holiday Inn Express are spacious and well-equipped, with free Wi-Fi, flat-screen TVs, and a work desk. The hotel also offers a

free breakfast for all guests and provides a relaxed environment with modern facilities.

Perfect For:
Families and groups who want budget-friendly accommodations with easy access to the city center and local attractions.

Unique Stays and Countryside Escapes
For those seeking a more unique and memorable stay, Canterbury and its surrounding countryside offer a range of charming and distinctive accommodations, perfect for a getaway or a special occasion.

1. The Barns at Langton
Located just outside Canterbury, The Barns at Langton offers a rural retreat that combines modern luxury with the charm of the countryside. This collection of converted barns offers stylish rooms and beautiful views of the surrounding countryside.

Key Features:

The rooms at The Barns are spacious and contemporary, with high ceilings and large windows. Guests can enjoy a peaceful escape in this quiet rural setting, and the property offers a lovely garden, perfect for relaxing after a day of exploration.

Perfect For:
Couples or anyone looking for a tranquil, rural retreat while still being within easy reach of Canterbury.

2. The Secret Garden Glamping

For something truly unique, The Secret Garden Glamping offers a glamping experience in the heart of the Kent countryside. The site features luxurious yurts and bell tents, offering guests a blend of nature and comfort.

Key Features:
Each glamping tent is fully furnished, with comfortable beds, heating, and even a private outdoor seating area. The glamping site offers a truly unique way to experience the Kentish

countryside, with easy access to Canterbury and the surrounding area.

Perfect For:
Those seeking an outdoor adventure with a touch of luxury, including couples or families looking for a unique and memorable experience.

3. Chilston Park Hotel

Located a short drive from Canterbury, the Chilston Park Hotel is set within a historic manor house surrounded by stunning gardens and parkland. This elegant property offers a taste of luxury in a country house setting.

Key Features:
The rooms are decorated in classic Georgian style, with antique furniture and views over the surrounding grounds. The hotel also offers a fine-dining restaurant, a spa, and a variety of outdoor activities, including tennis and walking trails.

Perfect For:

Those looking for a luxurious countryside escape with historical charm and plenty of activities to enjoy during their stay.

4. The Dairy at Tonge Barn

The Dairy at Tonge Barn offers a truly unique stay in a converted dairy barn on a private estate just outside Canterbury. With its contemporary design and rural setting, it's the perfect getaway for those seeking seclusion and luxury.

Key Features:
The Dairy is beautifully designed, with modern furnishings, a fully equipped kitchen, and an outdoor terrace overlooking the estate's grounds. It's ideal for couples or small families looking for a peaceful escape with easy access to Canterbury and the surrounding countryside.

Perfect For:
Those looking for a private, peaceful retreat in the countryside with luxurious amenities and a tranquil setting.

From charming boutique hotels and budget-friendly family accommodations to unique stays in the countryside, Canterbury offers a variety of options that cater to all tastes and budgets. Whether you're looking for a cozy B&B or a luxurious countryside escape, the city and its surroundings provide the perfect backdrop for a memorable stay.

CHAPTER EIGHT: OUTDOOR ACTIVITIES AND DAY TRIPS

River Stour Punting and Walking Trails

The River Stour is a defining natural feature of Canterbury, offering a serene environment for outdoor enthusiasts looking for an escape into nature. The river and its surroundings offer an ideal setting for punting, walking, and cycling. The river meanders through the heart of the city and the surrounding countryside, making it a perfect starting point for outdoor activities.

1. River Stour Punting

One of the most popular ways to explore Canterbury from a different angle is through punting on the River Stour. Traditional flat-bottomed punts allow you to gently glide along the river, offering a peaceful and scenic experience that provides stunning views of Canterbury's historic buildings and surrounding green spaces. Whether you are a first-timer or an experienced punter, this activity is relaxing and enjoyable.

Where to Punt:
Punting can be enjoyed along various stretches of the River Stour, particularly in areas close to the city center, where you can hire punts from operators near the city's medieval bridges. The best part of this experience is the tranquil atmosphere that surrounds you as you float past the city's lush landscapes.

Guided Tours:
If you prefer a more informative experience, several companies offer guided punting tours along the river. These tours are typically led by local guides who share insights about the city's history, the architecture you pass, and the significance of the river. The guided tours can also include stops at key landmarks and hidden gems that are difficult to access by foot.

Perfect For:

Couples, families, and history buffs looking for a relaxing and unique way to experience the city from the water. Punting is also great for nature lovers who enjoy peaceful outdoor activities in a picturesque setting.

2. Walking Trails Along the River Stour

Walking along the River Stour provides an excellent way to explore the natural beauty surrounding Canterbury. The Stour Valley Walk is one of the most popular routes that follows the river through picturesque villages, green meadows, and marshes. It offers a mixture of countryside and urban scenery, ideal for hiking and enjoying nature.

Key Routes:

The Stour Valley Walk: A long-distance trail that extends for over 60 miles, from the heart of Canterbury to the Suffolk coast. You can walk sections of the trail for a day trip or opt for a full hike.

Canterbury Riverside Walk: This circular route takes you around the River Stour, beginning at the city center and passing through the historic city and its surrounding meadows. This walk provides a wonderful opportunity to enjoy the peace and beauty of the river, while also taking in views of the medieval architecture and lush landscapes that line the banks.

Difficulty:
Walking along the river is accessible to walkers of all abilities. There are both easy and challenging sections, so you can choose a route that suits your preferences. The river is generally calm, and the paths are well-marked, making it a pleasant walk for families, casual hikers, and those with limited experience.

Perfect For:
Outdoor enthusiasts, families, and nature lovers. Whether you are looking for a leisurely stroll or a more challenging walk, there are options for everyone along the river.

Beaches and Nature Reserves Near Canterbury

The area around Canterbury offers a diverse range of outdoor activities, from relaxing days at the beach to exploring nature reserves and wildlife habitats. The natural beauty of the coastline and countryside makes Canterbury an ideal base for outdoor adventures.

1. Beaches Near Canterbury

Although Canterbury itself is not directly on the coast, it is within easy reach of some stunning beaches, each offering a different experience. Whether you are interested in a day of sunbathing, swimming, or simply enjoying the view, the nearby beaches are a perfect destination for a day trip.

Herne Bay

Herne Bay, located just 7 miles north of Canterbury, is a classic British seaside town with a long pebble beach and a Victorian pier. The beach is known for its peaceful atmosphere, making it ideal for a relaxing day by the sea. The town has a number of cafés, restaurants, and ice cream shops, providing a classic beach day experience.

Key Attractions:

Herne Bay is known for its Herne Bay Pier and Clock Tower, both iconic landmarks. The beach is family-friendly, and the town is home to various parks and gardens.

Activities:

In addition to enjoying the beach, you can walk along the pier, rent pedal boats, or cycle along the coast. There are also opportunities for birdwatching and nature walks along the coastline.

Whitstable

Just a short drive from Canterbury, Whitstable is a charming seaside town famous for its oysters and vibrant arts scene. The town's beach offers a mixture of shingle and sand, and it is well known for its beautiful sunsets. The coastline is lined with colorful beach huts, making it a perfect spot for photos.

Key Attractions:
Whitstable is famous for its Oyster Festival and thriving art galleries. The Harbour Street area is lined with shops, cafés, and seafood restaurants.

Activities:
In addition to sunbathing and swimming, visitors can try kitesurfing, go on boat trips, or enjoy the bustling waterfront. The town is also home to a number of galleries and art studios that highlight its creative culture.

Botany Bay (Broadstairs)
Botany Bay, located near Broadstairs (approximately 15 miles from Canterbury), is a stunning sandy beach surrounded by dramatic white chalk cliffs. The area is ideal for those who enjoy scenic beauty and a quieter, more relaxing atmosphere.

Key Attractions:
The cliffs and the dramatic coastline are perfect for photography. The beach is also ideal for picnics, and there are some small caves to explore along the cliffs.

Activities:
Botany Bay is known for its beautiful rock pools, perfect for children to explore. The beach is also great for swimming, sunbathing, and beach games.

Perfect For:
Families, couples, and nature lovers looking to spend a day relaxing by the sea or enjoying coastal activities.

2. Nature Reserves Near Canterbury

Kent is home to a number of nature reserves that offer a chance to explore the diverse ecosystems of the region, from wetlands and marshes to woodlands and heathlands.

Stodmarsh Nature Reserve
Stodmarsh Nature Reserve, located a few miles east of Canterbury, is a beautiful wetland area home to a variety of birds, including reed warblers, bitterns, and marsh harriers. The reserve consists of reedbeds, wetlands, and

floodplains, making it an ideal spot for birdwatching and nature walks.

Key Features:

There are several walking trails through the reserve, including a birdwatching trail and hidden hideaways for those who want to observe wildlife undisturbed. The site is also home to a rich variety of plant species and is particularly well-known for its wildflowers.

Perfect For:

Birdwatchers, photographers, and nature lovers who want to immerse themselves in Kent's diverse wildlife.

Blean Woods Nature Reserve

The Blean Woods near Canterbury is one of the largest areas of ancient woodland in southern England, with an extensive network of walking trails and opportunities for wildlife spotting. The area is particularly popular for its bluebells in the spring and its diverse range of flora and fauna.

Key Features:

The reserve has various walking routes, ranging from short strolls to longer hikes. The woods are home to a variety of wildlife, including deer, foxes, and a wide range of bird species.

Perfect For:
Hikers, nature enthusiasts, and families who enjoy woodland walks and outdoor activities.

RSPB Fairhaven Lake Nature Reserve

For those interested in birdwatching, RSPB Fairhaven Lake Nature Reserve, located on the edge of the city, offers a beautiful spot to explore the wetlands and watch for migrating birds. The area is home to a variety of waterfowl and other species, especially during the autumn and spring migrations.

Key Features:
The reserve features several walking trails, bird hides, and observation points. The lake is a particularly scenic spot, and the reserve offers a peaceful environment for nature walks.

Perfect For:
Birdwatchers and those seeking a tranquil escape into nature.

Excursions to Dover, Whitstable, and Chilham

Canterbury's location makes it an ideal base for exploring the wider Kent area, including the nearby towns of Dover, Whitstable, and Chilham. Each of these locations offers unique attractions, history, and activities that make them perfect for day trips.

1. Excursion to Dover

Dover is a historic port town located about 17 miles south of Canterbury, famous for its dramatic white cliffs, historic castles, and the Channel Tunnel.

Key Attractions:

Dover Castle: A large medieval fortress that has stood for over 2,000 years, offering panoramic views of the English Channel.

White Cliffs of Dover: Iconic cliffs that rise dramatically above the sea, offering breathtaking views and fantastic walking trails.

Dover Museum: Learn about the history of the town and its role in British maritime history.

Perfect For:
History buffs, hikers, and anyone interested in dramatic natural scenery.

2. Excursion to Whitstable
Whitstable is known for its oyster farming, charming beach, and lively atmosphere. It's an easy day trip from Canterbury, offering a laid-back, coastal retreat.

Key Attractions:

Whitstable Harbour: A lively area filled with restaurants, shops, and places to enjoy local seafood.
Whitstable Oyster Festival: A popular summer event celebrating the town's famous oysters.

Tankerton Slopes: Ideal for a scenic walk along the coastline.

Perfect For:
Food lovers, families, and anyone interested in experiencing the quintessential English seaside town.

3. Excursion to Chilham

A picturesque village located just a short drive from Canterbury, Chilham is known for its medieval architecture, including the Chilham Castle and charming streets.

Key Attractions:

Chilham Castle: A Grade I listed building with beautiful gardens and views over the surrounding countryside.
Chilham Village Green: A tranquil area perfect for a picnic or leisurely stroll.
The White Horse Inn: A traditional pub serving hearty meals in a quaint setting.

Perfect For:
Those looking for a peaceful village experience, history lovers, and anyone interested in medieval architecture and countryside walks.

With its diverse outdoor activities, scenic walking trails, and close proximity to coastal towns and nature reserves, Canterbury offers a wealth of options for those looking to explore the natural beauty of the region. Whether you're interested in punting on the River Stour, exploring the cliffs of Dover, or visiting charming villages like Chilham, Canterbury provides a range of outdoor adventures suitable for all types of travelers.

CHAPTER NINE: SHOPPING AND LOCAL FINDS

High Street Highlights and Independent Shops

Canterbury is not just a city steeped in history and culture but also a vibrant shopping destination. While the High Street features well-known national chains, it is the independent shops scattered throughout the city that truly make Canterbury a unique shopping experience. From boutiques and local designers to specialty stores offering artisan goods, there is something for every taste and interest.

1. Canterbury High Street

The High Street of Canterbury is home to a mix of traditional shops and modern stores, with the charming medieval architecture adding to the shopping experience. While you can find popular high-street brands such as Marks & Spencer, Boots, and Superdrug, the real appeal of the High Street lies in its independent offerings, which range from clothing boutiques to homeware stores.

Clothing Boutiques:
Several independent boutiques line Canterbury's High Street, offering fashionable clothing from local and international designers. Jigsaw Canterbury, for example, offers a range of high-end fashion for men and women, while The Wardrobe focuses on vintage and contemporary clothing pieces. Local shops like Jules B and Niche feature unique and stylish pieces, ensuring that visitors can find a one-of-a-kind outfit that cannot be purchased anywhere else.

Specialty Shops:
Canterbury's High Street is also home to specialty shops such as The Canterbury Cook Shop, which offers high-quality kitchenware and cooking essentials. The Greenhouse Café & Shop is another independent store that combines a delightful café experience with a selection of

eco-friendly homeware products, locally sourced goods, and organic treats.

Perfect For:
Those looking to explore trendy, independent fashion, local products, and artisanal home goods. The High Street is ideal for a day of leisurely shopping while admiring the city's historic setting.

2. St. Dunstan's and Northgate Shopping Areas

While the High Street is the heart of Canterbury's retail scene, areas like St. Dunstan's and Northgate offer additional opportunities to discover hidden gems and local treasures. St. Dunstan's is known for its charming independent bookshops, art galleries, and handcrafted jewelry stores.

The Art Shop & Gallery:
Located on St. Dunstan's Street, this independent store showcases a range of fine art and

contemporary paintings. It's an excellent stop for art lovers looking for a new piece to take home.

Canterbury Artisans:
Another independent shop located here, Canterbury Artisans specializes in showcasing handmade goods created by local artists and makers. From pottery to paintings, the shop features a rotating collection of works that reflect Canterbury's creative culture.

Perfect For:
Art enthusiasts, book lovers, and anyone looking for unique, handmade items that reflect Canterbury's rich artistic history.

Markets, Antiques, and Artisan Goods
Canterbury is well-known for its vibrant market scene, offering a mix of antiques, local produce, and artisan goods that are perfect for those who want to bring home something special from their trip. Markets are a central part of the city's cultural fabric, offering an authentic experience

where visitors can interact with locals and discover rare treasures.

1. Canterbury Market

Canterbury's Market Square is a focal point for traders selling a wide variety of goods, ranging from fresh produce to local crafts. This vibrant market takes place on Saturdays and provides a unique shopping experience where visitors can browse locally produced goods and artisanal items.

Local Produce:

One of the highlights of the market is the abundance of fresh produce available from local farmers and growers. Visitors can find a wide range of seasonal fruits, vegetables, cheeses, meats, and fresh bread. The market also features a selection of organic and specialty food products, perfect for foodies looking to take home some Canterbury flavors.

Artisan Goods:

The market is also home to a selection of handcrafted items from local artisans, including jewelry, ceramics, woodwork, and textiles. Many of these products are one-of-a-kind and represent the craftsmanship of Canterbury's local makers.

Perfect For:
Those seeking fresh, local produce or looking to buy a meaningful, handcrafted gift that represents the culture of Canterbury.

2. Canterbury Antique Shops

Canterbury is a haven for antique lovers, with a number of shops specializing in rare and vintage items. Whether you're looking for furniture, vintage clothing, or collectible memorabilia, there are several places in the city that cater to your needs.

Penny Farthing Antiques:
Located just a short walk from the High Street, Penny Farthing Antiques offers a collection of rare and vintage furniture, silverware, and artwork. The store is known for its extensive

selection of period pieces, making it a must-visit for anyone interested in high-quality antiques.

The Old Farmhouse Antiques:
This shop, located in the heart of Canterbury, specializes in French and English antique furniture and home décor. Whether you're interested in a stunning Victorian armoire or a unique antique mirror, this store offers something for every collector.

Perfect For:
Antique collectors, home decorators, and those seeking a historic, vintage item to take home.

3. Canterbury Artisan Markets
In addition to the general market, Canterbury also hosts various artisan markets throughout the year, typically offering a curated selection of handmade goods from local artists and crafters. These markets often coincide with local festivals or events and can be found in Canterbury's Guildhall or at Canterbury's Westgate Gardens.

Handmade Crafts:

These artisan markets feature an impressive selection of goods such as hand-blown glass, upcycled home décor, handmade candles, and local honey. The markets are an excellent way to discover unique items while supporting local craftsmen.

Seasonal Events:

Depending on when you visit, you might encounter Christmas markets or summer fairs, both of which feature a mixture of handmade crafts, seasonal produce, and locally sourced products that reflect the time of year.

Perfect For:

Travelers looking for authentic local crafts, seasonal items, or special gifts that celebrate the culture and spirit of Canterbury.

Souvenirs and Local Products to Bring Home

When visiting Canterbury, it's important to bring home something that truly represents the city and its heritage. Fortunately, the city offers a range of unique souvenirs and local products that make perfect mementos of your trip. From traditional Canterbury treats to locally sourced artisan products, there is something for everyone.

1. Canterbury-Specific Souvenirs

Canterbury Bells:
The Canterbury Bell, a type of flower native to the area, is a popular symbol of the city. Souvenir shops in Canterbury offer a wide selection of items featuring the Canterbury Bell motif, such as greeting cards, mugs, and tote bags. These items make for perfect, inexpensive mementos of your visit.

Canterbury Pewter:
For something more traditional, Canterbury Pewter produces high-quality pewter goods, including medals, plates, tankards, and commemorative spoons. These items often feature detailed engravings of famous landmarks or historical scenes from Canterbury.

Canterbury Cathedral Gifts:
The Canterbury Cathedral gift shop offers a wide range of souvenirs, including fine art prints, religious items, candles, and books related to the cathedral's history and architecture. Items from the Cathedral shop are both educational and meaningful for those with an interest in the city's most iconic landmark.

2. Local Food and Drink Products

Canterbury Lamb:
Known for its high-quality meat, Canterbury lamb is a delicacy in the region. Local butchers and food markets offer vacuum-sealed cuts of lamb for those who want to take home a taste of the countryside. You can also find Canterbury lamb in specialty food stores that focus on regional produce.

Kentish Ale and Cider:
Kent is known for its long-standing tradition of brewing, and Canterbury is no exception.

Numerous local breweries and cider houses produce excellent beverages. Local ales, such as those from The Canterbury Ales or The Kent Brewery, make for an authentic Canterbury souvenir. Additionally, the region's apple orchards produce some of the finest ciders, which you can buy in bottle or can for easy transportation.

Local Honey and Jams:
The region's rich agricultural heritage is reflected in the local honey and handmade jams produced by farmers and artisans around Canterbury. Look for honey flavored with local herbs or jams made from seasonal fruits grown in the Kent countryside, perfect for bringing home a taste of the region.

3. Handmade and Artisan Gifts

Canterbury Pottery:
Local potters create beautiful ceramic pieces, ranging from mugs and plates to decorative vases and bowls. These items make for great

gifts or home décor pieces, as they represent the craftsmanship of the region.

Local Woodwork:
Artisans in the Canterbury area create stunning wooden items such as cutting boards, coasters, and hand-carved utensils. These handmade pieces are often made from sustainable wood and are both functional and beautiful.

Perfect For:
Those looking for souvenirs that are functional, handmade, and reflective of Canterbury's local craftsmanship.

Conclusion
Canterbury offers an exceptional shopping experience, blending modern retail with the charm of independent shops and local artisan products. Whether you're strolling down the High Street, exploring antique shops, or hunting for locally made crafts, Canterbury provides a diverse range of options for all kinds of shoppers.

CHAPTER TEN: CONCLUSION: PLANNING THE PERFECT CANTERBURY ESCAPE

Sample Itineraries for Every Traveler

Canterbury offers an exciting array of experiences for every type of traveler. Whether you're in search of a peaceful getaway, an adventure through history, or a family-friendly exploration, there's an itinerary that can make your time in Canterbury truly unforgettable. Here are a few sample itineraries to cater to different travel styles, ensuring that you make the most of your time in this historic city.

1. The History Buff's Canterbury (2-3 Days)

Canterbury's rich heritage makes it a perfect destination for history lovers. From its Roman roots to its medieval grandeur, the city is a living history book. This itinerary is designed to immerse you in the key historical landmarks, museums, and educational experiences.

Day 1: The Historic Core

Morning: Begin your exploration at Canterbury Cathedral, a UNESCO World Heritage site. Spend at least two hours exploring this iconic landmark, including the crypt and the cathedral precincts.

Lunch: Enjoy a light lunch at a local café, such as The Goods Shed, known for its locally sourced ingredients and laid-back atmosphere.

Afternoon: Visit St. Augustine's Abbey and St. Martin's Church, both key historical sites in Canterbury. Take a guided tour if available, as these locations are crucial to understanding the spread of Christianity in England.

Evening: Explore the charming streets of Canterbury's Old Town, where you can enjoy a traditional British dinner at The Old Weavers restaurant, which sits along the banks of the River Stour.

Day 2: Archaeology and Medieval Walking Tours

Morning: Start with a visit to the Canterbury Roman Museum, where you can uncover the city's Roman past through interactive exhibits and a fascinating collection of artifacts.

Lunch: Head to The King's Head for lunch, offering hearty meals and historic charm.

Afternoon: Embark on a medieval walking tour of Canterbury, where a local guide will take you through the cobbled streets and tell tales of the city's medieval glory. Don't miss Westgate Towers, a remaining gatehouse from the medieval city wall.

Evening: Enjoy dinner at The Canterbury Tales, a family-friendly venue that brings to life Chaucer's classic tales.

2. The Nature and Outdoors Enthusiast (2-3 Days)

Canterbury is surrounded by natural beauty, from lush countryside to coastline, offering plenty of opportunities for outdoor activities. If you enjoy hiking, cycling, and nature exploration, this itinerary will help you discover the area's natural landscapes.

Day 1: River Stour Punting and Nature Reserves

Morning: Start your day with a relaxing river punt down the River Stour. This leisurely boat ride lets you take in the tranquil beauty of Canterbury from a unique perspective, surrounded by greenery and historic landmarks.

Lunch: Enjoy lunch at The Old Weavers or pack a picnic to enjoy in Greyfriars Garden, a quiet spot perfect for a break in nature.

Afternoon: Head to Blean Woods Nature Reserve for a peaceful walk or hike through ancient woodlands. The reserve is home to a wide variety of wildlife, and several well-marked walking trails offer the perfect way to explore this natural haven.

Evening: For dinner, visit The Crab and Winkle, a coastal pub offering locally sourced seafood in a cozy, rustic setting.

Day 2: Coastal Exploration and Day Trips

Morning: Take a day trip to Whitstable, a charming seaside town just a short train ride from Canterbury. Stroll along the seafront and enjoy a freshly caught seafood lunch at one of the town's acclaimed restaurants, such as The Crab & Winkle or Whitstable Oyster Company.

Afternoon: If time permits, take a short trip to the nearby Seasalter Nature Reserve for a coastal walk and bird-watching opportunities. Alternatively, head to Chilham, a picturesque village with scenic walking paths and views of the surrounding countryside.

Evening: Return to Canterbury and enjoy a cozy dinner at The Ambrette, a restaurant known for its Indian-inspired cuisine made with local ingredients.

3. Family-Friendly Canterbury (3 Days)

Canterbury is an excellent destination for families, with its mix of interactive museums, green spaces, and child-friendly attractions. This itinerary is designed to provide activities that will keep both adults and children entertained.

Day 1: Fun and Learning

Morning: Start with a visit to The Beaney House of Art & Knowledge, where families can explore interactive exhibits and hands-on activities. Kids will love the art, as well as the science and natural history displays.

Lunch: Stop for lunch at The Sandwich Shop, a family-friendly eatery with a great selection of sandwiches and snacks.

Afternoon: Head to Canterbury Roman Museum, where the whole family can explore the city's ancient past through fun, educational displays.

Evening: Enjoy dinner at Zizzi Canterbury, offering a child-friendly menu and casual, relaxed dining.

Day 2: Outdoor Adventures

Morning: Spend the morning at Dane John Gardens, a large public park where children can run around and play in the open green spaces. The gardens also have a maze, perfect for a little family challenge.

Lunch: Have a picnic in Westgate Gardens, another great spot for outdoor fun, followed by a stroll along the River Stour.

Afternoon: Visit Wildwood Trust, an animal sanctuary located just outside Canterbury, where kids can see a range of native British wildlife.

Evening: Return to Canterbury for a meal at The Chaucer, a family-friendly pub with a kid's menu and a welcoming atmosphere.

Day 3: Exploring Canterbury's Surroundings

Morning: Head to Howletts Wild Animal Park in the morning, an excellent wildlife park offering the chance to see rare animals such as elephants, tigers, and gorillas.

Lunch: Have lunch at the park's café, where you can relax after a fun-filled morning.

Afternoon: On the way back to Canterbury, stop by the Canterbury Heritage Museum, which offers plenty of child-friendly exhibits and activities.

Evening: End your family visit with a casual dinner at The Theatre Royal café, where you can unwind after an adventurous day.

Final Travel Tips and Seasonal Advice

Best Time to Visit: Canterbury is a year-round destination, but the most pleasant months for outdoor activities and exploring the city's historical sites are from April to October. Spring (April-May) and autumn (September-October) offer mild temperatures and fewer crowds, making these the ideal months for sightseeing. Summer (June-August) is also popular, but it can be crowded, particularly around major festivals. For those looking for winter charm, Canterbury's Christmas markets and festive lights in December provide a magical experience, although expect colder weather.

Getting Around: Canterbury is a compact city and is very walkable, with most major attractions within a short stroll from each other. For further exploration, consider renting a bike or taking public transportation. The train station is well connected to nearby coastal towns and cities, offering easy access to day trips.

Accommodation: Whether you prefer staying in the heart of the city or on the outskirts in a countryside retreat, Canterbury offers a wide variety of accommodation options, from charming boutique hotels to family-friendly lodgings. Booking in advance during peak seasons is recommended, as Canterbury can get busy, especially in the summer.

Local Etiquette and Cultural Tips: The British take punctuality seriously, so make sure to arrive on time for tours, reservations, and other appointments. Tipping in restaurants is customary but not mandatory, with around 10-15% being standard if service is good.

Travel Insurance: As always, it is advisable to take out travel insurance to cover any unforeseen circumstances during your trip, such as medical emergencies or cancellations.

Making the Most of Your 2025 Visit

Visiting Canterbury in 2025 provides an exciting opportunity to experience a mix of history, culture, and modern upgrades. Take advantage of the city's ongoing development, including the enhanced visitor centers and updated tourist information points, which will ensure a smooth and informed visit. Don't forget to check for special events and festivals taking place throughout the year, such as the Canterbury Festival, which typically takes place in October and features arts, performances, and local talent.

In conclusion, whether you're drawn to the rich history, natural beauty, family-friendly activities, or shopping scene, planning the perfect Canterbury escape is all about choosing the right mix of activities and experiences that suit your interests. With its unique blend of old and new, Canterbury offers something for every traveler.

Printed in Dunstable, United Kingdom